In the Comm...

At the Grocery Store

By Julia Jaske

I see shoppers
at the grocery store.

I see carts at the grocery store.

4 I see fruits at the grocery store.

I see cashiers at the grocery store.

I see vegetables
at the grocery store.

I see bread at the grocery store.

8 I see baskets at the grocery store.

I see baggers at the grocery store.

I see butchers
at the grocery store.

I see fridges at the grocery store. 11

I see stockers
at the grocery store.

I see scanners
at the grocery store.

Word List

grocery   cashiers   butchers

store   vegetables   fridges

shoppers   bread   stockers

carts   baskets   scanners

fruits   baggers

- I see shoppers at the grocery store.
- I see carts at the grocery store.
- I see fruits at the grocery store.
- I see cashiers at the grocery store.
- I see vegetables at the grocery store.
- I see bread at the grocery store.
- I see baskets at the grocery store.
- I see baggers at the grocery store.
- I see butchers at the grocery store.
- I see fridges at the grocery store.
- I see stockers at the grocery store.
- I see scanners at the grocery store.

CHERRY BLOSSOM PRESS

Published in the United States of America by Cherry Lake Publishing Group
Ann Arbor, Michigan
www.cherrylakepublishing.com

Book Designer: Keri Riley

cover: © Odua Images/Shutterstock; page 1: © Monkey Business Images/Shutterstock; page 2: © hedgehog94/Shutterstock; page 3: © ViDI Studio/Shutterstock; page 4: © BearFotos/Shutterstock; page 5: © Pressmaster/Shutterstock; page 6: © BearFotos/Shutterstock; page 7: © Aleksandar Malivuk/Shutterstock; page 8: © Drazen Zigic/Shutterstock; page 9: © Odua Images/Shutterstock; page 10: © FabrikaSimf/Shutterstock; page 11: © AlessandroBiascioli/Shutterstock; page 12: © Dusan Petkovic/Shutterstock; page 13: © hedgehog94/Shutterstock; page 14: © monticello/Shutterstock

Note from publisher: Websites change regularly, and their future contents are outside of our control. Supervise children when conducting any recommended online searches for extended learning opportunities.

Cherry Blossom Press is an imprint of Cherry Lake Publishing Group.

Library of Congress Cataloging-in-Publication Data

Names: Jaske, Julia, author.
Title: At the grocery store / written by Julia Jaske.
Description: Ann Arbor, Michigan : Cherry Blossom Press, 2023. | Series: In
 the community | Audience: Grades K-1 | Summary: "At the Grocery Store
 explores the sights and sounds of the grocery store. It covers people
 and objects found at the grocery store. Uses the Whole Language approach
 to literacy, combining sight words and repetition to build recognition
 and confidence. Simple text makes reading these books easy and fun.
 Bold, colorful photographs that align directly with the text help
 readers with comprehension"— Provided by publisher.
Identifiers: LCCN 2023003170 | ISBN 9781668927205 (paperback) | ISBN
 9781668929728 (ebook) | ISBN 9781668931202 (pdf)
Subjects: LCSH: Readers (Primary) | LCGFT: Readers (Publications).
Classification: LCC PE1119.2 .J36 2023 | DDC 428.6/2—dc23/eng/20230203
LC record available at https://lccn.loc.gov/2023003170

Printed in the United States of America
Corporate Graphics